Radiant

I0901819

LISA WILT

Radiant

An Advent Invitation *to* Grow *in the* Light *of* Christ

Abingdon Press
Nashville

Radiant:
An Advent Invitation to Grow in the Light of Christ

Copyright © 2026 Abingdon Press
All rights reserved.

No part of this work may be reproduced or transmitted in any form or by any means, electronic or mechanical, including photocopying and recording, or by any information storage or retrieval system, except as may be expressly permitted by the 1976 Copyright Act, the 1998 Digital Millennium Copyright Act, or in writing from the publisher. Requests for permission can be addressed to Rights and Permissions, The United Methodist Publishing House, 810 12th Avenue South, Nashville, TN 37203-4704 or emailed to permissions@abingdonpress.com.

Please note: Without in any way limiting the author's and Abingdon Press's exclusive rights under copyright, any use of this publication to "train" generative artificial intelligence (AI) technologies to generate text is expressly prohibited. The author and publisher reserve all rights to license uses of this work for generative AI training and development of machine learning language models.

Library of Congress Control Number: 2026942511
978-1-7910-4341-4

Scripture quotations, unless noted otherwise, are from the Holy Bible, New Living Translation, copyright © 1996, 2004, 2007. Used by permission of Tyndale House Publishers, Inc., Carol Stream, Illinois 60188. All rights reserved.

Continued on page viii.

Contents

Joy

Belonging

Hope

Continued from page iv.

Scripture quotations marked KJV are from The Authorized (King James) Version. Rights in the Authorized Version in the United Kingdom are vested in the Crown. Reproduced by permission of the Crown's patentee, Cambridge University Press.

Scripture quotations marked MSG are from THE MESSAGE, copyright © 1993, 1994, 1995, 1996, 2000, 2001, 2002 by Eugene H. Peterson. Used by permission of NavPress. All rights reserved. Represented by Tyndale House Publishers, Inc.

Cover description: Features a serene watercolor winter landscape of snow-covered evergreen trees glowing in the warm light of a low winter sun. Soft shades of blue, green, and gold blend across the sky while gently falling snow and sparkling points of light create a peaceful, contemplative atmosphere. The title, *Radiant,* appears in large copper-colored script across the center of the cover. Beneath it, the subtitle, *An Advent Invitation to Grow in the Light of Christ,* is presented in smaller light blue serif type, and the author's name, Lisa Wilt, appears below in gold uppercase letters. The spacious white foreground and luminous winter scene reinforce the Advent themes of hope, quiet reflection, and Christ's light shining through the darkness.

MANUFACTURED IN THE UNITED STATES OF AMERICA

Introduction

Advent is the season when God invites us to slow our breathing, quiet our hurry, and lean in close—something holy is rustling at the edges of our ordinary days. It's the time of year when heaven begins its gentle countdown, not with flashing lights or fanfare, but with a whisper: *Watch. Wait. Hope.*

This year, we enter Advent with a single word shimmering before us: **RADIANT**. Not the kind of radiance the world chases, but the glow that rises when God draws near. The radiance of promise. The radiance of a Savior wrapped not in gold, but in swaddling cloth. The radiance that warms the weary and steadies the fearful.

Like children tiptoeing toward the tree, trying to guess what's inside each wrapped box, we approach these days with a sacred curiosity. Advent is God's way of saying, "There is a gift coming—one you cannot rush, one worth the waiting."

Each candle we light is another corner of the wrapping paper lifted. Each Scripture reading is another hint of the miracle drawing near. And each day of this devotional becomes a small doorway, opening our hearts a little wider to the One who is already on His way—the One who makes every shadow shimmer with **radiant** hope.

Rest

November 29

Presence Over Perfection

Come close to God, and God will come close to you.
(James 4:8)

My hard-working dad always said, "A decent finish beats a perfect start." I think of that often during Advent—the season that invites me not to begin flawlessly, but to prepare faithfully.

Each year, my hope for Advent is spiritual growth. I long to draw closer to Christ as I wait for His coming, yet I'm easily distracted. When my Advent doesn't look as peaceful or prayerful as I imagined, discouragement creeps in. The perfect stretch of quiet time rarely appears. I tell myself I'll meet with God once the house is decorated, the gifts are bought, and my soul feels still.

But Advent reminds me that Jesus didn't wait for perfect conditions to come close to us. He entered a noisy world, a crowded town, a humble stable. If He didn't wait for silence, maybe I don't need to either. So I'm learning that any time is better than no time, and any place is better than no place. Noisy beats nothing. Sometime beats someday. A single candle still pushes back the dark.

Doing something about one thing—lighting a candle, whispering a prayer, opening Scripture for even a moment—helps me begin again. Time spent with God each morning quiets my noisy life. The storms around me may not be stilled, but the storms within me can be.

This Advent, I'm choosing presence over perfection, small steps over grand intentions, and simple nearness over elaborate plans. Christ is coming close. I want to come close too.

When and where do you most often meet with God in this season of holy waiting?

PRAYER

Lord, thank You that in this season of waiting, You are already here—ready and eager to meet with me. As I enter this sacred pause, help my heart to focus on Your coming light. Quiet my soul the way You quieted the world on that holy night in Bethlehem. Fill me with the hope, peace, joy, and love that Advent invites. I love You, Jesus. Amen.

November 30

Kisses for Baby Jesus

But Jesus said, "Let the children come to me. Don't stop them! For the Kingdom of Heaven belongs to those who are like these children."

(Matthew 19:14)

Some of my fondest Christmas memories are from when my kiddos were young and their eyes sparkled with radiant wonder. Our home was dressed in twinkling lights and treasured decorations. Snow globes were my son's favorite, and many had been lovingly recategorized from "untouchable" to "okay to touch—but be careful." My daughter delighted in stringing pearl garland on the lower branches of the tree, then around herself, and then back on the tree again.

One snowy afternoon, we walked through our neighborhood, boots crunching beneath us, when Alyssa suddenly stopped. Her eyes widened. "Look, Mommy, dat's BABY JESUS!" she exclaimed, pointing to a life-sized plastic manger scene on a neighbor's porch. With the enthusiasm of a tiny explorer, she bounded across the lawn and up to the figures, leaving her footprints behind.

My first instinct was to call her back. But what harm could she do?

Before I could speak, she gently picked up the plastic baby and cradled Him in her arms, rocking Him, kissing Him. Then came hugs for Mary and Joseph—whom she adoringly called "JoeJoe." She was filled with wonder.

And so was I.

In that moment, Alyssa reminded me what it meant to approach Jesus with childlike faith. No hesitation. No formality. Just pure affection and awe. This season, may we pause long enough to remember the Christ Child. May we cradle Him in our hearts, offer Him our love, and let wonder lead us to worship.

How might you cradle Christ in your heart this season—with affection, awe, or quiet worship?

Prayer

Jesus, thank You for radiant memories that still warm my heart. Let Your light shine through my remembering. May childlike wonder stir fresh joy in me, and may I reflect Your glory in every tender moment this season. Amen.

December 1

Advent's Upside-Down Greatness

But among you it will be different. Those who are the greatest among you should take the lowest rank, and the leader should be like a servant.

(Luke 22:26)

Some sermons linger like your grandma's Christmas casserole—warm, comforting, and seasoned just right for the soul. One of my pastors, Ashley Morgan-Kirk, recently preached one of those messages on servanthood, delivered with the clarity of a star over Bethlehem. She reminded us that while the world is obsessed with being the GOAT—the greatest of all time—Jesus invites us into something far more countercultural: becoming the LOAT, the least of all time. Yes, LOAT. Let go of becoming the greatest; lean into becoming the least.

Advent is the perfect season to hear this. It's the time when we wait for a King who arrives in the most unkinglike way imaginable. While the world looks for greatness wrapped in gold, God sends greatness wrapped in swaddling clothes. While we chase platforms and applause, Jesus chooses a manger throne. Advent whispers that God often comes quietly, slipping into the ordinary places we overlook.

Jesus didn't just preach LOAT living—He embodied it from His first breath. The King of kings became an infant. The Creator of the universe needed to be carried. The Light of the world entered through the dim doorway of a stable. The One who holds all things together was held in Mary's arms. In God's upside-down kingdom, greatness looks like service, and humility becomes the doorway to joy.

So this Advent, let's embrace the LOAT invitation. Let's love quietly, serve faithfully, and choose presence over performance. Because in heaven's hall of fame, the least aren't forgotten—they're celebrated.

Where might God be inviting me to step out of the GOAT race and quietly practice LOAT living this week?

Prayer

Lord Jesus, as we wait for Your coming, quiet our striving and soften our hearts. Teach us to choose humility over hurry and service over status. Make room in us for Your light. Let our small acts of love prepare a manger for Your presence this season. Amen.

December 2

Russell Stover Bloopers

He will take delight in you with gladness.
With his love, he will calm all your fears.
He will rejoice over you with joyful songs.
(Zephaniah 3:17b)

I was born in the farming community of Mattoon, Illinois, but Kansas City is where my soul has settled and taken root. KC is a city that knows how to celebrate—fourtime Super Bowl champs, a city with the spray of fountains second only to Rome in number, and barbecue joints that are world-renowned. From crafting cards at Hallmark to building the first stadium designed for women's pro sports, KC doesn't just show up—it shows heart.

It also happens to be the international home of Russell Stover Chocolates—home to a century of sweet traditions. And during Advent, when the world feels wrapped in twinkle lights and anticipation, one of my favorite treats comes in a humble little box: the Bloopers. Inside are chocolates that didn't pass inspection—misshapen, smudged, or fused together like cousins at a family reunion. And yet, they're still delightfully rich and perfectly sweet.

In this season of waiting, they remind me of Zephaniah's gentle promise in today's reading that God delights in you and me. Advent isn't about presenting a polished version of ourselves to the coming King. It's about bringing our blooper moments, our smudged attempts, our fused-together days to the One who arrives not because we are perfect, but because we are loved.

Christ comes into a world that is uneven, unfinished, and a little messy—much like those chocolates. And still, He delights. He sees beauty in our blemishes, worth in our weariness, hope in our half-formed offerings. We are not mistakes; we're sweet masterpieces in the making, shaped by the hands of a God who refuses to discard us.

So as you light the candles this Advent—hope, peace, joy, love—remember this: God sings over you. Not because you're flawless, but because you're His. And in this season of holy anticipation, that is more than enough.

When has someone else's blooper given you hope to keep going?

PRAYER

Lord, thank You for loving me through every misstep. As Advent light grows, let hope rise in me—quiet and steady. Help me see beauty in imperfection and grace in growth. Use my stumbles to remind me I'm still chosen, still Yours. Let Your coming joy pour out, quiet my doubt, and carry me forward. Amen.

December 3

Jesus Never Asked for Salami Roses

But the Lord said to her, "My dear Martha, you are worried and upset over all these details! There is only one thing worth being concerned about. Mary has discovered it, and it will not be taken away from her."

(Luke 10:41-42)

Advent has a way of exposing our inner Martha. I used to dust my plants before guests arrived—shining their leaves like they were auditioning for a *Better Homes & Gardens* Christmas spread. No joke. Now, I'm so laid back I shove clutter into the laundry room, close the door, and declare it off-limits with a smile. I look back at my obsession with detail and laugh—and maybe cringe a little.

During Advent, when we're supposed to be preparing room for Christ, we often end up preparing rooms for company instead. We overstress, overplan, and overthink, inviting others into our homes until hospitality feels less like a joy and more like a December performance review. Suddenly, we're fussing over the charcuterie board—arranging meats and cheeses like we're curating a museum exhibit. But here's the thing: Jesus never asked for a charcuterie board with gourmet salami made to look like roses. Not at Christmas. Not ever.

There's a world of difference between entertaining and hospitality. Entertaining says, "Look at me." Hospitality says, "I see you." Entertaining is a stage—lights, camera, perfection. Hospitality is a table, dusty or not, where connection is served. Martha was busy with the details, flustered by the fuss. Mary sat at Jesus's feet, soaking in His presence. And during Advent, that's the invitation: presence over presentation. Jesus didn't scold Martha for caring; He simply reminded her that one thing mattered most. And that "one thing" is the heartbeat of Advent: Emmanuel—God with us.

So let's get off the Mary-and-Martha teeter-totter and plant our feet on the solid ground of grace-filled welcome. When we shift from performance to presence, our homes become havens. The pressure lifts. The soul exhales. And suddenly, the chipped Christmas mug and mismatched stockings don't matter—because love is being served. And who knows? That guest you welcome with a simple meal and a listening ear might be more than they appear. Hebrews 13:2 reminds us: "Don't forget to show hospitality to strangers, for some who have done this have entertained angels without realizing it!"

How might choosing presence over perfection help you notice Emmanuel—God with us—in the ordinary moments of your day?

PRAYER

Lord, during this holy season, teach me to welcome with grace, not grandeur. Quiet my striving for perfection and open my heart to presence. May my home reflect Your love—not through spotless floors or fancy meals, but through warmth, listening, and peace. Help me serve connection over performance and see each guest as a gift from You. Amen.

December 4

Rest in the Manger

Christ is the visible image of the invisible God. . . .
He existed before anything else,
and he holds all creation together.
(Colossians 1:15a, 17)

Advent is a season of leaning forward with hope toward the God who comes close. I traveled to the Holy Land recently with my church family. One of my favorite places captures that longing perfectly: the site where Jesus was born, tucked beneath the Church of the Nativity. Below the altar, steep steps lead into a sacred grotto where the entrance is so low every visitor must bow to enter. In Advent, that posture becomes our practice. Humility becomes the doorway, not just the posture. To enter, stiff necks must bend just as hearts must bend to behold the miracle God wrapped in flesh over two thousand years ago.

On that Bethlehem night, the world's story turned a page with the cry of a newborn. Eternity's compass quietly recalibrated in the silence of a manger. No fanfare. Just straw and surrender. Advent reminds us that God often arrives this way—quietly, gently, in places we least expect.

But this isn't just cosmic poetry—it's deeply personal. Jesus didn't come to dazzle empires. He came to heal raw hearts experiencing real struggles; to mend families torn by anger, abuse, and addiction; to hold together the pieces we've dropped while trying to carry everything. He is still the One who steadies us when grief grips tightly, when schedules overwhelm, and when prayers feel unanswered.

And through it all, He remains the same—the thread that ties our past, present, and future with love that never unravels. Advent invites us to rest in that truth. When life feels off-kilter and the frantic "to-dos" outnumber the peaceful "ta-da" moments, we can stop striving and start surrendering. Rest isn't weakness—it's wisdom. It's the sacred pause that whispers, "I don't have to hold it all together, because He already does."

So today, as candles flicker and carols rise, I choose to remember the One who was wrapped in cloth and laid in straw. I may not know what tomorrow holds, but I know the One who holds tomorrow, and that is enough for today.

How might you rest this Advent, trusting Jesus to carry what you can't?

PRAYER

Jesus, You were born into the fragility of straw, and yet You hold the world in Your hands. I'm tired of trying to manage what was never mine to carry. Be my anchor when peace feels far and my strength when the load is too heavy. I give You my tangled "to-dos" and trust that You are enough—for tomorrow and for today. Amen.

December 5

Presence in the Waiting

That is why I tell you not to worry about everyday life—whether you have enough food and drink, or enough clothes to wear. Isn't life more than food, and your body more than clothing? . . . So don't worry about tomorrow, for tomorrow will bring its own worries. Today's trouble is enough for today.

(Matthew 6:25, 34)

"Be where your feet are." This Southern saying beautifully captures the art of being fully present in the moment. And during Advent, the season of holy waiting, its wisdom shines even brighter.

Advent invites us to slow down, hush the noise, and lean into expectancy. But silencing the buzz of worry and soaking in each moment takes intentionality. Living fully means wringing every drop of wonder from each breath and trusting God with what's ahead, even when the calendar fills and the to-do lists multiply.

Ironically, I still have work to do on this. Often, I feel like I'm straddling two worlds—one foot anchored on the dock of faith, while the other hovers in tomorrow's dinghy of worry, uncertain and unsteady. Advent exposes this tension: the already and the not yet, the promise and the waiting, the hope and the heaviness.

Yet Jesus showed us how to live with complete presence and trust. Long before shepherds heard angels sing, long before wise men followed a star, His life was marked by being exactly where He needed to be—fully engaged, fully surrendered, fully present. His footprints are etched across history, and even our calendar testifies to His authority. We count our days based on the day of His birth, and yet He invites us to make every day count by walking with Him.

Advent reminds us that God stepped into our world not in a rush, but in perfect timing. When we stay present, trusting Him with the future, He brings peace to our hearts and meaning to our moments. Being where our feet are allows us to experience God's grace fully, even in life's struggles. With Emmanuel—God with us—every step matters.

When do you struggle most with being fully present and peaceful?

PRAYER

Lord, during this Advent season, help me be fully present in every moment. Teach me to lay my worries at Your feet and trust You through every worrisome trial. With You by my side, Emmanuel, I can be where my feet are and be at peace. I am grateful for Your presence, Your promises, and the hope You bring into the world. Amen.

Joy

December 6

Four Thousand Reasons to Delight

Taste and see that the Lord is good.
Oh, the joys of those who take refuge in him!
(Psalm 34:8)

Advent invites us to slow down and savor—not just the season, but the Savior. In these weeks of waiting, watching, and wondering, God gently reminds us that He designed us for delight. Using just two words, I can give you nearly four thousand reasons why I believe this: taste buds.

God gave you and me almost four thousand taste buds, each packed with sensory cells that renew every single week. As a pharmacist, I can tell you: Taste is the least necessary of our five senses for survival. We could live without it. We could nourish our bodies without ever savoring a thing. But God didn't create us to merely survive. He created us to delight. Taste exists not out of necessity but out of divine generosity.

During Advent, when flavors fill our homes—cinnamon, peppermint, cocoa, citrus—I'm reminded that God could have made nourishment bland and functional. Instead, He made it joyful. He made it renewing. He made it something we anticipate, just like we anticipate Christ's coming.

I enjoy eating—a lot. And Advent only heightens that joy. Still, any gift can be misused, which is why Paul grounds us with his reminder in 1 Corinthians 10:31: "So whether you eat or drink, or whatever you do, do it all for the glory of God." Advent feasting is not about excess; it's about awareness. It's about tasting with gratitude, savoring with worship, and letting every bite point us back to the Giver.

What foods bring you the most delight? How might each taste become a tiny Advent reminder of God's goodness breaking into your day?

Prayer

Lord, today I pause to taste and see Your goodness. You've filled my life with flavor, joy, and grace. As I wait for Christmas, help me savor each moment—not rush past it. Let every bite, every breath, every blessing remind me of Your presence. May my heart be a manger, ready to receive You. In this season of anticipation, awaken my senses to delight in You daily. Amen.

December 7

Joy in the Middle of Our Mismatched Mornings

This is the day the Lord has made.
We will rejoice and be glad in it.
(Psalm 118:24)

The countdown to Christmas is on—candles lit, calendars opened, and hope humming somewhere between the coffee pot and the crumpled covers. I've woken up (yes, that is the right verb tense, even if it sounds wrong) beside the same man for nearly forty years. And in all that time, one thing has remained gloriously consistent: My husband and I don't just sleep on opposite sides of the bed—we wake up on opposite sides of the attitude spectrum.

I'm the "Good morning, Lord!" type. He's more of a "Good Lord, it's morning" kind of guy. I rise cheerfully optimistic. He rises realistically pessimistic.

And yet—here's the Advent miracle—hope meets us both. One bright-eyed, one bleary-eyed, but both greeted by the same sunrise, the same mercy, the same God who steps into our ordinary mornings with extraordinary grace.

Because Advent is exactly that: God slipping into our yawning, stretching, stumbling-into-the-day humanity. The truth is, we all wake up somewhere between optimism and pessimism. (A "poptimist," perhaps?) Life is a dramedy, a sacred blend of laughter and lament, cocoa and chaos, carols and cracked-open hearts. But today's Scripture reminds us that no matter how we rise, the day itself is a gift. And rejoicing? That's not a mood. It's a choice. A daily Advent practice.

If your morning mood had an Advent soundtrack, what would it be, and how might hope help invite God into that melody, even if it's jazzed-up grumbling?

PRAYER

Lord, thank You for mornings—messy hair, mismatched moods, and all. Whether I rise with praise or need Your grace to get there, remind me this day is Yours. Let hope be my wake-up call. Shape my heart with joy, patience, and a smile that reflects You during this holy season of Advent. Amen.

December 8

Donut Holes and Tears

Weeping may last through the night,
but joy comes with the morning.
(Psalm 30:5b)

Advent is the season when our deepest longings meet God's steady promise of light. During the holy and hushed season, darkness and dawn can coexist. Grief and joy can share the same breath.

One moment you're laughing at a silly reel, and the next, a scent brings tears. For me, it's the smell of donuts. My dad enjoyed them often, especially warm maple squares. After he left for heaven, we honored him the best way we knew how: by sharing donuts with our church family in our hometown of Mattoon, Illinois. In his obituary, we invited people to enjoy a donut hole and do a kind deed in his memory. He would've loved that.

Now, at family gatherings, we raise a donut hole after grace and toast to Dad. Even our grandson joins in, turning what could be sorrow into a sweet celebration. It feels a little like Advent: grief softened by hope, sadness brightened by a small but certain joy.

Hope-filled grief reminds us of the love we still carry, while joy reminds us that love never ends. Scripture doesn't ask us to choose between sorrow and joy—it invites us to hold both. "Our hearts ache, but we always have joy" (2 Corinthians 6:10). And "Be happy with those who are happy, and weep with those who weep" (Romans 12:15).

Advent whispers the same truth: Emmanuel—God with us—steps into both our tears and our laughter. He doesn't wait for us to feel only joy or only sorrow.

He comes close to us right where the two mingle. So today, if you miss someone, celebrate them in a way that would make them smile from heaven. Light a candle. Say their name. Share their favorite treat. Because sometimes, the best way to honor those we love is with a laugh—and maybe a donut. Hope rises with the remembering.

How can we find joy and hope in the midst of grief and challenges, trusting that God is always present?

PRAYER

Loving God, in this Advent waiting, meet me in both sorrow and joy. When my heart aches, remind me that grief is love enduring, and joy is Your promise that healing is near. Help me honor those I miss with kindness and hope. Let Your presence rise like dawn. You are my hope, my comfort, and my peace. Amen.

December 9

Your Favorite Holiday Outfit?

The Spirit of the Lord God is upon me...to give unto them beauty for ashes, the oil of joy for mourning, the garment of praise for the spirit of heaviness.

(Isaiah 61:1, 3a KJV)

Isaiah's words feel like a wardrobe God lays out for us each morning. We all have favorite outfits, especially around the holidays. The ones we keep at the front of the closet. The ones we reach for without thinking because they make us feel like ourselves—confident, comfortable, seen.

Advent reminds me that God knows we reach for familiar garments too—especially when life feels heavy. But instead of ugly Christmas sweaters, He offers us something better:

- Beauty for ashes
- Oil of joy for mourning
- A garment of praise for the spirit of heaviness

These are the clothes of the coming Christ. These are the garments of the One who stepped into our world wrapped not in royal robes but in swaddling clothes.

And just like our favorite outfits, these garments fit us perfectly. They accent God's strength rather than our flaws. They help us stand tall in hope. They make us comfortable resting in His steadfast love.

During Advent, when the world feels hurried and our hearts feel stretched, the garment of praise becomes our softest sweater—warming us, steadying us, reminding us that joy is not something we manufacture. It's something we receive. So, as we wait for Christmas, we don't wait empty-handed. We wait clothed—wrapped in the promises of Isaiah 61, wrapped in the presence of Emmanuel.

How might wearing a garment of praise shift the way you move through this Advent week?

PRAYER

Lord, clothe me today in what only You can give. Trade my ashes for Your beauty, my heaviness for Your praise, my mourning for Your deep and steady joy. Wrap me in Emmanuel's presence so I walk confident in Your love. Dress my heart for Advent hope, and let Your peace be the garment I carry into the world. Amen.

December 10

The Milk and Cookie Rule

"Open your mouth wide, and I will fill it with good things."
(Psalm 81:10b)

When my children were young, we had what we called the milk-and-cookie rule: "You have to drink a glass of milk with every cookie." My daughter accepted the rule with a smile, while my son protested with great drama, insisting, "I want another cookie, but my tummy can't hold more milk."

No one likes rules, and no one likes being told no. Something about being denied makes us want the thing even more—especially when it's sweet. And honestly, exercising self-control is hardest when we're hungry.

During Advent, I'm reminded that hunger isn't always physical. Sometimes I'm hungry for affirmation, and instead of turning to God, I reach for lesser things. I go to my phone before I go to the Father's throne. I look to Facebook "likes" instead of looking into His Book, where I'm already affirmed as His beloved child.

Advent invites me to slow down, to wait, to prepare room. It's a season that gently redirects my hunger. Just as the milk-and-cookie rule helped my children make room for the nourishing things first, spending time in God's Word before spending time in the world helps me make room for the One my soul is truly hungry for.

This Advent, I want to choose the better portion—to fill up on the milk of His Word before reaching for the cookies of distraction. I want to make room for Him, not just in my schedule, but in my desires, my habits, and my heart.

What unhealthy cravings do you have that crowd out soul-nourishing practices?

Prayer

Jesus, as I savor the sweet treats of this season, help me practice holy restraint. Prepare my heart to make room for what truly nourishes my body, mind, and soul as I await Your coming. Thank You for the wisdom to choose what leads me closer to You. Amen.

December 11

Every Good and Perfect Gift

Whatever is good and perfect is a gift coming down to us from God our Father, who created all the lights in the heavens. He never changes or casts a shifting shadow.

(James 1:17)

Count me in for every good and perfect gift—especially in Advent, when the world slows just enough for us to notice the sparkle of God's generosity. As we wait for the arrival of Jesus, the Light of the World, I find myself craving gifts like:

- Buttery popcorn and a feel-good movie
- Compliments like "Have you been working out?"
- The scent of fresh evergreen beside a crackling fire
- Being told, "I just want you to know that you are the best friend ever"
- Dinner at my favorite restaurant with family
- Little plastic cups of ice cream with flat, wooden spoons, eaten with children
- S'mores and songs around a flickering campfire
- The sound of a child giggling in anticipation as they shake gifts under the tree
- Hearing "I luv you" from my child

How might the simple gifts you're savoring this Advent become reminders of God's unchanging goodness in a world full of shifting shadows?

PRAYER

Lord, thank You for every good and perfect gift You've placed in my life—the little things, the big things, and the quiet in-between things. In this Advent season of holy waiting, open my eyes to Your beauty all around me, and let every light, every kindness, and every moment of joy point me back to Jesus, the Light who never dims and the Gift who never stops giving. Tune my ears to hear Your melodies of grace as I wait with hope. Amen.

December 12

Christmas Pillows and Snowflakes

God's glory is on tour in the skies,
God-craft on exhibit across the horizon.
Madame Day holds classes every morning,
Professor Night lectures each evening.

Their words aren't heard,
their voices aren't recorded,
But their silence fills the earth,
unspoken truth is spoken everywhere.
(Psalm 19:1-4a MSG)

Christmas deco pillows make me smile. You'll find them all over my home because new pillows can brighten an old couch. (I have three of those.) Pillows are an inexpensive way to decorate for the holidays, and during Advent, they feel especially fitting—little reminders that something new and beautiful is coming.

Recently, my daughter introduced me to pillow covers, which means I can expand my collection without storing entire pillows. My husband still doesn't understand the purpose of pillows that aren't to be used. He prefers function over style, yet some things don't have to serve a function. They simply bring beauty and joy to our lives.

Advent works the same way. God tucks beauty into our days, not because it's "useful," but because it stirs our hearts to hope. Even better than pillows, God gives us sunsets and snowflakes. Sunsets don't need to be beautifully breathtaking. And snowflakes don't need to be one-of-a-kind pieces of crystalline art, but they are. God gives us the northern lights that dance and paint the night sky with curtains of color. These glimpses of beauty are like Advent whispers—small signs that the Light of the World is drawing near.

Beauty brings joy. God showers us with beauty because He wants us to be joyful as we wait. He loves us dearly. And here on earth, He gives us a foretaste of the beauty to come in heaven, where every color, every sparkle, every joy will be complete.

What has our Creator created that brings you joy?

PRAYER

Lord, as pillows brighten our homes, awaken my heart to Your beauty. Let every sunset and silent wonder whisper that Christ is near. Fill my waiting with joy, my days with hope, and my spirit with awe at Your coming Light in this holy season of gentle promise. Amen.

Belonging

December 13

Singing with the Radio

I'd say you'll do best by filling your minds and meditating on things true, noble, reputable, authentic, compelling, gracious—the best, not the worst; the beautiful, not the ugly; things to praise, not things to curse. . . . Do that, and God, who makes everything work together, will work you into his most excellent harmonies.

(Philippians 4:8b-9 MSG)

When I'm singing Christmas carols along with the radio in my car, I think I sound good. But when the music stops, I hear the truth: I'm wildly off-key. Advent exposes that same reality in my soul. When I try to live without the Spirit's steadying melody, I slip into discord. I complain, I grumble, I rush, and I push forward instead of pausing to wait on God.

Advent reminds us that we were never meant to live life a cappella. We were meant to live accompanied, guided by the Spirit, who tunes our thoughts, tempers our reactions, and softens the sharp edges of our impatience.

Advent becomes God's gentle invitation to stop singing solo. It invites me to stop striving and to stop pretending I can hold the melody on my own. The One we're waiting for—the One wrapped in swaddling clothes—came precisely because we can't make our own music.

Jesus enters our off-key world and brings harmony where there was only noise. He tunes our hearts to hope again. He aligns our lives with His peace. He restores rhythm to our days and grace to our relationships. This Advent, instead of trying harder, we can listen deeper. We can let the Spirit accompany us, steady us, and shape us into a song that sounds like Christ.

What areas of your life most need to be worked into excellent harmonies with the Holy Spirit's help?

PRAYER

Jesus, in this season of waiting, I need Your steadying presence. My days often feel rushed or out of rhythm. Thank You for stepping into my off-key moments with Your peace and for sending people who lift me when I'm weary. Tune my heart to hope, align my steps with Your grace, and help me bring harmony to others. Amen.

December 14

A Rich Life

"Give away your life; you'll find life given back, but not merely given back—given back with bonus and blessing. Giving, not getting, is the way."

(Luke 6:38 MSG)

I love free gifts and unexpected bonuses. Advent feels like both. It's the season when heaven leans close and whispers, "Get ready—abundance is coming." Today's verse carries that same promise: an invitation to a life that overflows. Generosity becomes the secret ingredient, the quiet miracle that multiplies joy.

During Advent, I'm reminded that everything I have belongs to God. I'm simply a steward of my time, talents, and treasures, waiting—like Mary, like the shepherds—for God to reveal how He wants them used. And when I release my grip, my soul flourishes.

Life rarely unfolds as planned. In high school, I dreamed of becoming a writer; my father dreamed of me becoming a pharmacist. God, in His perfect timing, wove both dreams together. After decades of serving in pharmacy, I now write—newly retired and in awe of His design. Advent teaches me that God's timing is never rushed, never late, always purposeful.

Perhaps your life too looks different from what you imagined. Advent reminds us that dreams don't flourish by chasing our own goals alone. Growth takes root when we align with God's priorities—when we wait, listen, and follow His lead. He flips the world's wisdom: to lead is to serve; to be lifted is to lift others; to flourish is to help others thrive.

Scripture echoes this truth—Elijah passed his cloak to Elisha, and Moses gave his staff to Joshua. Rahab sheltered spies, and Elizabeth uplifted Mary. Barnabas poured into Paul, who then guided Timothy. Each act of giving reflects a kingdom principle: God's way is not about grasping but offering. Advent is the season that proves it—God so loved the world that He gave. In giving, we find life abundant. In offering what we have, our hearts align with Him. And in this season of holy anticipation, we remember: God often births His biggest miracles through our smallest yeses.

What little dreams might become big realities if you were to dream big and give big this Advent?

Prayer

Lord, in this season of holy anticipation, teach me the joy of generous living. Loosen my grip so my hands may offer what You entrusted to me. Align my dreams with Your perfect timing. Birth abundance through my small yeses, and let my giving reflect Your heart. Make my life a quiet miracle of overflowing grace. Amen.

December 15

Porch Pirates or Blessing Bandits?

The world of the generous gets larger and larger;
the world of the stingy gets smaller and smaller.
The one who blesses others is abundantly blessed;
those who help others are helped.
(Proverbs 11:24-25 MSG)

During Advent, we wait for the greatest Gift ever given—Jesus, God's generosity wrapped in swaddling clothes. As we light candles and count down the days, we're reminded that God didn't hold back. He came near. He came small. He came for us.

And maybe that's why this season is the perfect time to rethink the stories we hear about porch pirates. We all know the ones—people who sneak up to steal packages. Some of us have even watched our own deliveries disappear. But what if, during Advent, we flipped the script?

What if instead of porch pirates who take, we became Advent blessing bandits who give? Like a secret Santa with a holy twist, we could leave a small gift on someone's step, ring the doorbell, and dash away with joy. Advent reminds us that light breaks into darkness quietly, unexpectedly, beautifully. Our kindness can do the same.

Scripture tells us that generosity boomerangs. When we bless others, blessing finds its way back to us. So what do you have—right now, in this season of giving—that could become a small Advent miracle for someone else?

- Maybe that oversized holiday fruit basket delivered to your doorstep is more than your family can enjoy, and you could share a few fruits with a neighbor.

- Maybe your evergreen branches or winter berries are offering a few festive clippings you could bundle and deliver as a simple seasonal blessing.
- Maybe you have a recipe you could double—banana bread, chili, cookies—and you could leave a portion on someone's porch as a quiet Advent surprise.
- Maybe your child has outgrown clothes that would be perfect for a family with littler ones.

Advent is a season of holy anticipation. As we wait for Christ, we can also watch for opportunities to scatter kindness like confetti.

How have you been blessed by a neighbor? How might you start a wave of Advent kindness by becoming a blessing bandit?

PRAYER

Lord Jesus, Generous Gift wrapped in humility, enlarge our hearts this Advent. Make us quiet bearers of Your light, slipping kindness onto doorsteps and hope into weary souls. Teach us to give freely, trusting Your boomerang blessing. As we wait for You, help us scatter grace like confetti and become Your holy blessing bandits in a world hungry for wonder. Amen.

December 16

Believe and Belong

You say you have faith, for you believe that there is one God. Good for you! Even the demons believe this, and they tremble in terror.

(James 2:19)

Advent reminds us that the longest faith journey may still be the twelve inches from our head to our heart. Many of us believe deeply, and yet we watch those we love step away from the faith that shaped our lives. We know God with our minds and trust Him with our hearts, but they may not. And that gap can feel wider than twelve inches; it can feel like a canyon.

Today, so many in the younger generation call themselves "Nones"—not because they believe in nothing, but because they check "None" when asked about religion. Others are "Dones"—not hostile, just weary. They've seen hypocrisy, felt pressure, or longed for something gentler than what they experienced. They're not rejecting God as much as they're stepping back from what felt confusing or heavy. And for parents and grandparents who love Jesus and love their kids, this reality can sit like a stone on the heart.

But here's the Advent good news: God isn't checking boxes. He's lighting candles. He's not asking our children for perfect theology or flawless attendance. He's drawing near—cradle-close—to them just as He once drew near to us. Emmanuel—God with us—came not to be acknowledged but to be received, and He knows exactly how to meet each wandering heart. Even when our kids seem far, He is not. Even when they're unsure, He is steady. Even when they're done, He is not done.

Advent hands us hope like a warm cup between cold fingers—hope that faith is ultimately about relationship, not labels; hope that even if our children wander, God never does; hope that their hearts still have a home; hope that belonging to Him brings peace, purpose, and grace in His timing, not ours. This season reminds us that God specializes in quiet arrivals, slow dawns, and unexpected homecomings.

So whether someone you love is a "None," a "Done," or simply sorting through life with more questions than answers, take heart: The God who came as a baby still comes close. He sees them. Loves them. Wants them. And He holds your longing too. Advent invites us not only to believe in Him, but to trust that the ones we love most are never beyond His reach. That's where hope starts humming.

Where might God be inviting you to trust Him again with the heart of someone you love?

PRAYER

Lord, hold those we love close, even when they feel far from faith. Quiet our fears and steady our hope as You gently draw their hearts toward Your light. Teach us to trust Your timing, love them well, and rest in Your nearness. Let Advent awaken hope for every wandering soul. Amen.

December 17

Emmanuel in the Empty Spaces

You go before me and follow me.
You place your hand of blessing on my head.
Such knowledge is too wonderful for me,
too great for me to understand! . . .
If I ride the wings of the morning,
if I dwell by the farthest oceans,
even there your hand will guide me,
and your strength will support me.
(Psalm 139:5-6, 9-10)

I've heard it said that being alone is a physical state of being, while being lonely is a mental state.

And while I understand the difference, both can feel excruciating, especially around the holidays. Loneliness cannot be quieted by the company of a loud TV. It cannot be drowned out by Christmas carols on the radio. Loneliness feels like it can swallow us whole. It hurts. It feels heavy. It can make us feel helpless and hopeless.

During Advent, these feelings can even sharpen. The world sparkles with lights and gatherings, yet our hearts may feel dim or quiet. But Advent is also the season that whispers a deeper truth: God steps into our loneliness. He comes close. He draws near in the waiting.

Honestly, I struggle with feelings of loneliness even though I know those feelings are not facts. The fact is this: You and I are never alone. Emmanuel—God with us—is not just a name we sing in December. It is a promise stitched into every ordinary day. He is the breath that fills our lungs and the hope that fills our hearts.

Advent reminds me that God often does His most tender work in the quiet, in the stillness, in the moments when I feel most alone. Daily, He is teaching me that being alone with Him is rich soil for spiritual growth. I can be alone and not be lonely, because the One who came as a baby in Bethlehem still comes to meet me in the silence.

When has God used quiet alone time with Him to speak to you?

PRAYER

Lord Jesus, in this Advent waiting, I sometimes feel lonely, yet I know I am never alone. In the holy stillness, speak to me. While the world vies for my heart, I offer it to You. Come, Lord Jesus, come. My heart is listening. Amen.

December 18

My Shepherd

God, my shepherd!
I don't need a thing.
You have bedded me down in lush meadows,
you find me quiet pools to drink from.
True to your word,
you let me catch my breath
and send me in the right direction.

Even when the way goes through
Death Valley,
I'm not afraid,
when you walk at my side.

(Psalm 23:1-4a MSG)

Here in Kansas City, we may not see shepherds, yet every Advent their quiet faithfulness returns to my mind as they stand watch in our family nativity scene. I love the story about two ministers who met a shepherd boy in Wales; he was hearing impaired and couldn't read.

They explained that Jesus wanted to be his shepherd, to always look after him just as he looked after his sheep. They taught him to repeat the words "The Lord is my shepherd," using the fingers and thumb of his right hand to help him remember. Starting with his thumb and then a finger for each of the five words, they taught him to pause at the fourth word, *my*, remembering, "This promise was meant for me."

Years later, when back on the moors of Wales, one of them asked about the shepherd boy. The previous winter, there had been terrible storms, and the young shepherd boy had been buried in a snowdrift with his sheep. The villager who was telling the story said, "When his body was discovered, he was holding the fourth finger of his right hand."

The young boy was clinging to his shepherd. This story brings tears to my eyes and brings Psalm 23 to life. When we feel cold and buried, we can remember that "the Lord is *my* shepherd." He is our personal shepherd.

How does knowing you have a personal shepherd make you feel?

PRAYER

Lord Jesus, my Shepherd-King, thank You for staying near in this season of waiting. When I feel cold or alone, surround me with the warmth of Your promised coming. Let Your light rise in my heart and guide me through the shadows. Teach me to wait with trust, hope, and quiet joy as You draw near this Advent. Amen.

December 19

The Beauty Behind the Ugly Gift

The people that walked in darkness have seen a great light: they that dwell in the land of the shadow of death, upon them hath the light shined.

(Isaiah 9:2 KJV)

I'm staring at the ugliest gift I've ever been given. It's big and clunky, made of hard black plastic. But my now-grown son gave it to me. I hot-glued a small olive wood cross from the Holy Land onto the corner, hoping to redeem its appearance. Still unattractive. Still enormous. Still blocking my window. Yet it's the most useful gift I've ever received.

It's my mammoth computer monitor—secondhand, lovingly selected, and proudly delivered by my tech-savvy son. Garrett was thrilled to give me this early Christmas present. As he rearranged my desk, scooting my cute lamp aside to make room for the eyesore, I swallowed the urge to shout, "IT'S TOO BIG!" I thanked him, smiled, and quietly planned to dismantle the monstrosity the moment he returned to college.

But something happened over Christmas break. What I had seen as a gift I didn't want became a gift I loved. Researching Scripture while writing became easier. I could keep multiple windows open. My eyes weren't as strained. My work flowed. My son was right. Bigger was better. Ugly was useful.

And suddenly, this clunky black rectangle became an Advent teacher. Advent is full of unexpected gifts—holy things wrapped in ordinary packaging. A Messiah arriving in a feeding trough. A King wrapped in rags. Salvation was delivered through what looked small, unimpressive, and even inconvenient. Israel longed for a warrior; God sent a baby. They wanted a throne; God gave a manger. The first Christmas gift didn't look like what anyone wanted, but it was exactly what the world needed.

Just like today's verse reminds us, it's hard to consider ugly trials "pure joy." It's hard to believe anything good can come from the dark, the clunky, the unwanted. But Advent whispers the truth: God transforms what looks unlovely into something life-giving. The ugly becomes useful in His hands. The unexpected becomes the very thing that saves us. He did it in Bethlehem. He does it in our lives. He always does.

When have you received something from God that you didn't want at first, but later realized you needed?

Prayer

Lord, thank You for gifts that arrive in shapes I don't expect. When life feels clunky, unwanted, or unlovely, open my eyes to the light You are already shining. Teach me to trust Your timing, Your wisdom, and Your transforming love. Turn every "too big" burden into a blessing that draws me closer to You. Amen.

Hope

December 20

Hope Is Like Snow

I pray that God, the source of hope, will fill you completely with joy and peace because you trust in him. Then you will overflow with confident hope through the power of the Holy Spirit.

(Romans 15:13)

Living in Kansas City, we don't just dream of white Christmases—we often wake up to them! And when that first snow falls, it's like heaven decided to toss bright hope across our brown lawns.

Now, my yard isn't winning any landscaping awards. It's got crunchy brown grass mingled with bare spots. But when snow covers it all? Ta-da! The mess disappears under a blanket of dazzling white, and suddenly, everything sparkles.

Hope is a lot like that.

When we're in the messy middle—raising kids on fumes, sweating through job frustrations, or just trying to keep the laundry from staging a coup—hope doesn't erase the hard stuff. But it sure makes it more beautiful. It reminds us that what we see isn't all there is. That God is still working, still present, still good.

Hope doesn't demand perfection. Today's verse gently whispers, "There's more to come." It covers our weary places with grace and gives us strength to keep going. Like snow on a tired lawn, hope transforms what's dry and dormant into something dazzling.

So if your life feels a little brown and brittle right now, don't lose heart. Hope is in the forecast. And when it falls, it won't just change how things look—it'll change how you see. Even a single flake of hope can shimmer in the sun.

What part of your life feels brown and brittle and could use a fresh covering of hope?

PRAYER

Lord, when life feels dry and dormant, cover me with Your hope. When I feel worn out or overlooked, help me remember that Your hope transforms everything. Remind me that You're still working, even when I can't see it. Let Your peace settle over my heart like fresh snow—quiet, gentle, and full of promise. Thank You for being the source of joy, even in winter seasons. May even my smallest "Amen" echo in heaven and shimmer with trust. I choose to believe You're making all things new. Amen.

December 21

FROM GLORY TO GLORY

> *Nothing between us and God, our faces shining with the brightness of his face. And so we are transfigured much like the Messiah, our lives gradually becoming brighter and more beautiful as God enters our lives and we become like him.*
>
> *(2 Corinthians 3:18 MSG)*

Advent is the season when we remember that Jesus came once in a manger, comes now into our everyday messes, and will come again in glory. Advent invites us to watch for the Light and to let that Light do its transforming work in us.

No matter what bad you do, God won't love you any less. No matter what good you do, God can't love you more. You are His child, fully loved right now—but he loves you too much to leave you stuck, alone with your old self, wanting to change but not knowing how to make change stick.

Advent reminds us that we don't transform ourselves. The Light comes to us. Our Savior wants us to live fully free. He came to save the lost and the lonely. And sometimes—especially in this season of hurry, pressure, and expectations—we need to be saved from ourselves.

Left to my own volition, I fret and worry. I can be self-serving and rude when I'm in a hurry. I can be greedy and gluttonous when I'm hungry. I can be cocky and cantankerous when things don't go my way. And I like to be right, especially in arguments.

When I try to accomplish life on my own, I fall short. But when I keep my eyes fixed on Jesus—the One we wait for, the One who is already here—He fixes me and my bad attitude. Advent is the season when we remember: The Light has come, and the Light is still coming.

Today's scripture says it best. We gradually become brighter and more beautiful as we are transformed into His image with ever-increasing glory. Advent is not just about waiting for Jesus to shine—it's about letting Him shine through us.

How might you shine brighter and look more like Jesus today?

PRAYER

Jesus, Light of the World, please help me to be irresistible like you. Let my life glow with your presence. Help me attract others with my soul-smile. I want my eyes to dance so others wonder about my secret—the source of my pure joy. You are my joy, Jesus. Your love is magnetic. As I wait for you this Advent, draw me closer and make me brighter. Amen.

December 22

Hope That Silences Hurry

"Look at the birds, free and unfettered, not tied down to a job description, careless in the care of God. And you count far more to him than birds."

(Matthew 6:26 MSG)

It's been said by many that worry doesn't empty tomorrow of its sorrow; it empties today of its strength. I agree. Worry is a conversation we have with ourselves about things we cannot change, while prayer is a conversation we have with God about things He can change.

During Advent, this contrast becomes even more vivid. Advent is the season of holy waiting—waiting with hope instead of worry, expectation instead of exhaustion, trust instead of tight-fisted control. Perhaps this is why Jesus tells us to look at the sparrows. They don't plant or harvest or store food in barns, yet God feeds them even when everything looks frozen and barren in winter. In today's reading, He reminds us that we are treasured. We are more cherished than birds and more beautiful than flowers.

Advent whispers the same truth: The God who once came in a manger still comes into our mess. The God who once wrapped Himself in flesh still wraps us in care.

God doesn't want us to worry. He wants us to be carefree in His care. He wants us to rest in His provision, His love, and His attention to detail. Worrying is natural. Trusting our Heavenly Father is supernatural. And Advent is our yearly reminder that supernatural trust is possible because God keeps showing up.

What worries do you find hardest to give to God? How has He proven that He is trustworthy?

PRAYER

Lord, quiet my rushing heart. Teach me the sparrow's trust and free me from worry's grip. In this season of holy waiting, help me rest in Your provision, Your presence, and Your tender care. Let hope rise, silencing hurry, as I welcome You into every detail of my day. Amen.

December 23

Good Grief?

No eye has seen, nor ear heard, nor the heart of man imagined, what God has prepared for those who love him.
(1 Corinthians 2:9)

Many days, I feel like Charlie Brown, perpetually followed by a gloomy rain cloud. When sadness overwhelmed him, he would famously groan, "Good grief." At first glance, "good" and "grief" seem like an odd pairing—two words that don't belong together. This paradox became real to me right before Christmas, when I lost my dad. Shortly after the holiday, we laid him to rest during what was the coldest week Kansas

City had seen in eighty years, with wind chills plunging to −40 degrees. The bitter cold seemed to deepen the sting of an already heart-wrenching week. While I'm profoundly grateful for the promise of heaven, the ache of missing my dad remains. Grief is hard. It hurts.

My father lived a long life, for which I am thankful; yet not all fathers have the same number of years. In our church family, we recently faced the heartbreaking loss of a dad who went to heaven before his son started kindergarten. Moments like this make us cry out to God, "Why?"

There's nothing that feels good about grief. And yet, the Bible offers a healing balm for grieving hearts: hope. Christ transforms our grief from hopeless to hope-filled. Just as oxygen fills our lungs, hope fills our souls. While grief is heavy, God's promises of eternal life are good. Today's Scripture reminds us that heaven is a place without grief, where goodness reigns. One day, I will see my dad again and feel his warm hug. And so will you be reunited with those you love who have gone on to heaven.

When does grief hit you hardest?

PRAYER

Abba Father, when grief feels heavy, making it hard to breathe, please remind me of Your promises that fill my soul with hope. I look forward to seeing You and my loved ones in heaven. Thank You for taking the fear of death and replacing it with the hope of heaven. Amen.

December 24

Hope Redecorates Our Hearts

"You must not covet your neighbor's house."
(Exodus 20:17a)

For twenty-four years, I lived in the practical home my husband bought before we were married—solid brick, dark wood, basic trim, and small windows. Built in the 1970s, it was energy-efficient. Dave loved function over what he deemed "foo-foo." Our home was outdated, and when I saw stylish homes on HGTV, I grew sad with envy. I longed for light and airy spaces—very different from my reality.

Advent is a season of longing, but not the kind that spirals into comparison. Envy never brings joy and rarely feels good. God knows this. That's why "You shall not covet" made God's top-ten list. Coveting is sneaky—it disguises itself as sadness, frustration, discontentment, or even misplaced resentment.

But Advent reminds us of this hope: God doesn't shame us for longing—He redirects it. He invites us to name it, tame it, and trade it for something better. Before the Light of the World stepped into the darkness, God's people waited with honest hearts. We can too. Truthfully, we have to name our sin before we can tame it with the help of the Holy Spirit.

Covering up coveting doesn't make it disappear, and getting what we want doesn't always satisfy. Paul reminds us in 1 Timothy 6:6, "But godliness with contentment is great gain" (KJV). Contentment brings peace—a fruit of walking with His Spirit. Coveting only steals it.

This Advent, I'm learning to let joy and gratitude lighten and brighten my home instead. Hope reminds me that beauty isn't just found in open floor plans or natural light—it's found in open hearts and Spirit-filled lives. Christ came to dwell with us, and His presence is the truest light any home can hold.

Where and when do you struggle most with contentment, and how might Advent hope help you see your life through a lens of gratitude today?

Prayer

Lord Jesus, Light of the World, enter the dim corners of my heart this Advent. Redirect every longing that drifts toward comparison. Replace envy with gratitude, discontent with Your peace, and shadowed thoughts with Your radiant presence. Redecorate my spirit with hope, so my life becomes a dwelling warmed by Your coming grace. Amen.

December 25

When the Light Breaks In

The light shines in the darkness,
and the darkness can never extinguish it.
(John 1:5)

When my children were young, Christmas Eve shimmered with anticipation. Their little bodies wiggling with pure, unfiltered joy as we set out one cookie along with a plate full of baby carrots for Santa and his reindeer—because even Santa needed his vegetables. After pouring him a tall glass of milk, we'd curl up together to read the story of baby Jesus's birth.

Then I'd tuck them in snug and warm, hoping sleep would find them quickly so I could hide the gifts for our family's favorite tradition—a Christmas morning scavenger hunt.

Morning would arrive soon with the first light of dawn, when they'd hop out of bed to discover what treasures Santa had left during the dark of night. They knew dawn was coming, and they couldn't wait!

This Christmas morning, you may find yourself excitedly ready to open presents, enjoy a big family dinner, and celebrate the birth of Jesus. Or perhaps your day will be a time of quiet reflection, even loneliness. No matter how your day unfolds, God's message to you is the same—morning has come, and the Light of Heaven has broken in!

We have spent Advent preparing, praying, and anticipating the coming of the Messiah. And now He is here—and that changes everything! The same Light that broke into the world that first morning in a manger in Bethlehem still continues to shine. Here. Now. In you.

The birth of Jesus is not just a moment to celebrate—it's an invitation to receive. To receive the Light that brings peace in place of striving. Joy in the midst of uncertainty. A Savior who is not far off, but close by. This is the wonder of Christmas: God did not remain distant or abstract. He came near, wrapped in vulnerability, placed within reach.

Where do you see the Light of Christ breaking into your life today?

PRAYER

Thank You, God, for the gift of this day and the light of Your Son. Thank You that Your light shines in every place—bringing hope, peace, and joy. As I celebrate today, help me to receive all that You have given. Let Your light fill my heart, guide my steps, and overflow into the lives of those around me. Remind me that Your presence is near, Your love is steady, and Your light will never fade.

More from Lisa Wilt

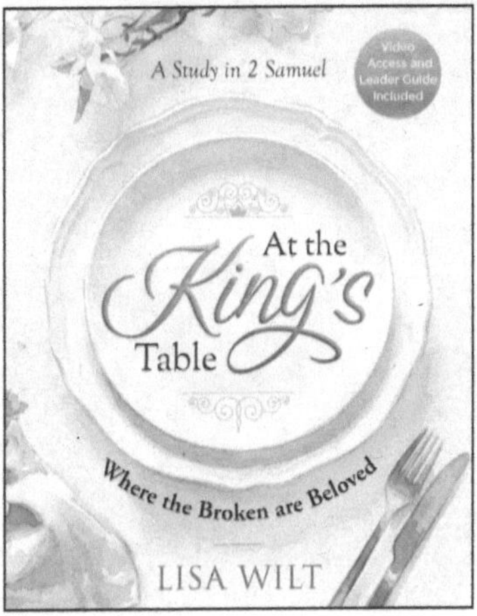

Grace has already pulled out a chair for you.

In *At the King's Table,* Lisa Wilt invites you into the tender and transformative story of Mephibosheth in 2 Samuel, a forgotten prince carried from hiding to honor and given a seat at the king's table. This six-week study speaks directly to women who have ever felt overlooked, invisible, or less than, offering a healing vision of a God who doesn't wait for us to fix ourselves. Through Scripture, reflection, and guided questions, you'll discover a God who seeks you out, calls you by name, restores you from your lowest places, and covers your wounds with grace. At the heart of this study is a simple and life-changing truth: even in the places where you feel broken, you are cherished, chosen, and invited to sit with the King.

Learn more at:
abingdonwomen.com
/bible-studies/at-the-king-s-table

www.ingramcontent.com/pod-product-compliance
Lightning Source LLC
La Vergne TN
LVHW032255040926
847296LV00035B/448
9781791043414